I0605725

INSIDE THE NFL

PHILADELPHIA EAGLES

by Charlie Beattie

An imprint of Abdo Publishing
abdobooks.com

ABDOBOOKS.COM

Published by Abdo Publishing, a division of ABDO, PO Box 398166, Minneapolis, Minnesota 55439.
Copyright © 2026 by Abdo Consulting Group, Inc. International copyrights reserved in all countries. No part of this book may be reproduced in any form without written permission from the publisher. Abdo & Daughters™ is a trademark and logo of Abdo Publishing.

Printed in China.
052025
092025

Cover Photos: Kathryn Riley/Getty Images Sport/Getty Images (Jalen Hurts); Focus on Sport/Getty Images (Reggie White)
Interior Photos: Kara Durrette/Getty Images Sport/Getty Images, 4–5; Perry Knotts/Getty Images Sport/Getty Images, 6; Mitchell Leff/Getty Images Sport/Getty Images, 7; Cooper Neill/Getty Images Sport/Getty Images, 8, 11 (top), 11 (bottom), 61 (top right); Gregory Shamus/Getty Images Sport/Getty Images, 9, 54; Michael Owens/Getty Images Sport/Getty Images, 10; Abdo Publishing, 12–13, 58; AP Images, 14–15, 22, 30; Bettmann/Getty Images, 16, 17, 24–25, 27, 37; Walter Stein/AP Images, 18; Sporting News Archive/Getty Images, 19, 26 (bottom), 60 (top); Vic Stein/Getty Images Sport/Getty Images, 20, 23; Bruce Bennett Studios/Getty Images Studios/Getty Images, 21, 60 (bottom left); David Durochik/AP Images, 26 (top); New York Daily News Archive/Getty Images, 29; Corbis/Bettmann Archive/Getty Images, 31; Focus on Sport/Getty Images, 32 (top), 38, 40 (top); Jeff Moreland/Icon Sportswire/Getty Images, 32 (bottom); Mario Suriani/AP Images, 33; James Drake/Getty Images Sport/Getty Images, 34–35, 60 (bottom right); G. Paul Burnett/AP Images, 36; Focus on Sport/Getty Images Sport/Getty Images, 39; Paul Spinelli/AP Images, 40 (bottom); Damian Strohmeyer/AP Images, 41; Kevin Terrell/AP Images, 42; Paul Spinelli/NFL Photos/AP Images, 43; Otto Greule Jr./Allsport/Getty Images Sport/Getty Images, 44; Doug Pensinger/Getty Images Sport/Getty Images, 45, 48, 61 (top left); Al Bello/Getty Images Sport/Getty Images, 46–47; Sporting News/Getty Images, 49 (top), 63; Ezra Shaw/Getty Images Sport/Getty Images, 49 (bottom); G. Newman Lowrance/AP Images, 50; Ron Jenkins/AP Images, 51; Jonathan Daniel/Getty Images Sport/Getty Images, 52; Rich Graessle/Icon Sportswire/Getty Images, 53, 61 (bottom); Aaron M. Sprecher/AP Images, 55, 56; Ryan Kang/AP Images, 57; Elsa/Getty Images Sport/Getty Images, 59

Editor: Rebecca Higgins
Series Designer: Laura Graphenteen
Production Designer: Katharine Hale

Library of Congress Control Number: 2024948462

Publisher's Cataloging-in-Publication Data

Names: Beattie, Charlie, author.
Title: Philadelphia Eagles / by Charlie Beattie
Description: Minneapolis, Minnesota: Abdo Publishing, 2026 | Series: Inside the NFL | Includes online resources and index.
Identifiers: ISBN 9781098296872 (lib. bdg.) | ISBN 9798384919391 (ebook)
Subjects: LCSH: Philadelphia Eagles (Football team)--Juvenile literature. | National Football League--Juvenile literature. | Football teams--Juvenile literature. | American football--Juvenile literature.
Classification: DDC 796.33264--dc23

CONTENTS

Eagles defensive tackle Milton Williams (93) sacks Chiefs quarterback Patrick Mahomes during Super Bowl LIX on February 9, 2025.

CHAPTER 1

SUPER DEFENSE

SUPER BOWL LVII HAD BEEN AN INSTANT CLASSIC. ON FEBRUARY 12, 2023, the Philadelphia Eagles and the Kansas City Chiefs slugged away at each other for 60 minutes, piling up a total of 73 points. It was one of the highest-scoring Super Bowls ever. But Kansas City got the last laugh. The Chiefs hit a field goal in the final seconds to win 38–35.

Two years later, the teams met in a rematch at Super Bowl LIX on February 9, 2025. By then, Chiefs quarterback Patrick Mahomes had become a National Football League (NFL) legend. He'd led the team to three championships, including the last two. Many expected him to come through again in Super Bowl LIX. This time, however, the Eagles wanted revenge.

REBUILT

Through 11 games of the 2023 season, the Chiefs and the Eagles looked to be headed for a Super Bowl rematch. The Chiefs were 8–3, while the Eagles were flying at 10–1. But things soon fell apart in Philadelphia. The Eagles dropped five of their last six games and lost in the first round of the playoffs.

The biggest reason for the team's collapse was a poor defense. The Eagles ranked 26th out of 32 NFL teams in yards allowed. They ranked 30th in points. General manager Howie Roseman decided to make some changes. The team already had some stars, such as defensive tackle Jalen Carter and cornerback Darius Slay. To boost the unit, Roseman signed new middle linebacker Zack Baun. The Eagles also used their first two draft choices on cornerbacks Quinyon Mitchell and Cooper DeJean.

The Eagles gave up 426 yards in their 32–9 playoff loss to the Tampa Bay Buccaneers on January 15, 2024.

The changes helped right away. Suddenly, the Eagles were a defensive force. Only one team allowed fewer points in 2024. No one allowed fewer yards. The new additions played big roles in the turnaround. Baun was an All-Pro in 2024. Mitchell finished second in the voting for the Defensive Rookie of the Year Award. Despite starting only nine games, DeJean finished fourth.

The rebuilt defense complemented a potent Eagles offense. Quarterback Jalen Hurts threw for 18 touchdowns and rushed for 14 more. Meanwhile, powerful running back Saquon Barkley ran for a league-leading 2,005 yards.

READY TO SOAR

Eagles fans filled the Superdome in New Orleans for Super Bowl LIX. Their team had charged through the playoffs, winning their games by 12, 6, and 32 points. Yet the Chiefs came into the game as slight favorites. Though they'd won an NFL-best 15 games, the Chiefs hadn't overpowered teams as they had in prior years. Still, Mahomes always seemed to play his best in the biggest

Eagles cornerbacks Quinyon Mitchell, *left*, and Cooper DeJean, *right*, combined for three interceptions and a fumble recovery in Philadelphia's four playoff games after the 2024 season.

moments, and many predicted he would find a way to come through in the clutch again.

Philadelphia forced a quick punt on the Chiefs' first possession. Then the Eagles did it again on Kansas City's second and third drives. Altogether, Kansas City had gained just 26 yards. And when Eagles kicker Jake Elliott ended the next drive by booting a 48-yard field goal through the uprights midway through the second quarter, Philadelphia already led 10–0. There was no celebration yet, though. As Mahomes jogged back on the field, everyone knew these were the moments he lived for.

Two Eagles defenders take down Kansas City's star tight end Travis Kelce in Super Bowl LIX. Philadelphia held Kelce to four catches for 39 yards.

Eagles wide receiver DeVonta Smith catches a touchdown pass during Super Bowl LIX.

NOT SO FAST

The Chiefs took over at their own 30. Mahomes dropped back on the first play. Eagles linebacker Josh Sweat burst into the backfield. Mahomes tried to step away, but Sweat grabbed the quarterback's shoulder and pulled him down for a 4-yard loss. Mahomes tried another pass on second down. Sweat and rookie linebacker Jalyx Hunt burst through. They dropped the Chiefs star for a 3-yard loss.

The Eagles had forced a third-and-16. This time, Mahomes rolled to the far side of the field. As he scrambled, DeJean moved toward the sideline. All the way, the rookie followed the quarterback's eyes. DeJean knew that Mahomes might force a pass back toward the middle. It was a dangerous play. But Mahomes was known to take risks.

When Mahomes threw across his body, DeJean was ready. He cut in front of the receiver and intercepted the ball in stride. He raced back toward the other side of the field as the Chiefs' offense gave chase. He made it to the sideline near the Kansas City end zone. He then planted and cut back. Two Chiefs linemen were there, but neither could get a hand on DeJean. He crossed the goal line, then wheeled back to celebrate with his teammates. "I was running around like a little kid," DeJean said later. "I didn't have any celebrations planned."

"I WAS RUNNING AROUND LIKE A LITTLE KID. I DIDN'T HAVE ANY CELEBRATIONS PLANNED."

—COOPER DEJEAN

COMPLETING THE ROUT

Elliott added the extra point after DeJean's pick six for a 17–0 lead. That was still the score when Kansas City took over at its own 6 with 1:49 left in the half. Though the Eagles had shut down Mahomes all half, he still had time to get points on the board. Philadelphia knew that could change the dynamics of the second half in a big way.

Mahomes took the snap in the shotgun formation. Standing on his own goal line, the quarterback was bumped as he tried to throw over the middle, where Baun was waiting. As the ball came low to his right, Baun lunged. The linebacker made a spectacular diving interception, extending his arms to pull the ball in at the 14.

Players pour Gatorade on Eagles head coach Nick Sirianni near the end of Super Bowl LIX.

Philadelphia quarterback Jalen Hurts holds the Vince Lombardi Trophy after Super Bowl LIX.

Two plays later, Philadelphia's offense put the finishing touch on an incredible half. Quarterback Jalen Hurts lobbed a 12-yard touchdown pass to receiver A. J. Brown. The Eagles took a 24–0 lead into the break. They had allowed the Chiefs only 23 total yards. Thanks to a pair of interceptions by two of the team's new faces, the Super Bowl rout was on. Philadelphia went on to win 40–22 to claim the team's second Super Bowl title.

BIRTHDAY BOYS

Cooper DeJean was celebrating his 22nd birthday on Super Bowl Sunday in 2025. But he wasn't the only Eagle who had a spectacular birthday. The team's star running back, Saquon Barkley, turned 28 on the day of the game. Barkley finished with 57 yards rushing and 40 receiving yards as he won a Super Bowl title for the first time.

Eagles running back Saquon Barkley had a team-high six pass receptions in Super Bowl LIX.

NFL TEAMS MAP

NFC EAST

NFC WEST

NFC NORTH

NFC SOUTH

AFC

AFC EAST

- BUFFALO BILLS
- MIAMI DOLPHINS
- NEW ENGLAND PATRIOTS
- NEW YORK JETS

AFC WEST

- DENVER BRONCOS
- KANSAS CITY CHIEFS
- LAS VEGAS RAIDERS
- LOS ANGELES CHARGERS

AFC NORTH

- BALTIMORE RAVENS
- CINCINNATI BENGALS
- CLEVELAND BROWNS
- PITTSBURGH STEELERS

AFC SOUTH

- HOUSTON TEXANS
- INDIANAPOLIS COLTS
- JACKSONVILLE JAGUARS
- TENNESSEE TITANS

Bert Bell, *white shirt*, talks to Eagles players in 1939. Bell coached Philadelphia from 1936 to 1940 in addition to owning the team.

CHAPTER 2

FLY EAGLES FLY

JUST FOUR YEARS AFTER THE NFL WAS FOUNDED IN 1920, THE FIRST Philadelphia-based NFL team took the field. The Frankford Yellow Jackets made a big impression. In 1926, the team based in the northeast Philadelphia neighborhood of Frankford was an NFL champion. But by 1931, the Yellow Jackets were gone. With the country in the midst of the Great Depression (1929–1939), Frankford ran out of money and had to stop operating.

In 1933, an ambitious former college quarterback named Bert Bell bought what was left of the Yellow Jackets and formed a new team. Bell was thrilled to own a franchise. "All I ever wanted to be was a football man," he later said. The new owner ditched the local Frankford location and rebranded his team for all

> ***"ALL I EVER WANTED TO BE WAS A FOOTBALL MAN."***
>
> ***—BERT BELL***

of Philadelphia. At the time, President Franklin Roosevelt's "New Deal" economic plan was in full swing to pull the country out of the Great Depression. The symbol of the New Deal was an eagle. In a nod to the program, Bell named his new team the Eagles.

TWO-MAN SHOW

Even with the soaring nickname, the Eagles didn't take flight in their early years. Bell and his business partner, Lud Wray, had barely any money to operate a team. To cut costs, they did almost everything themselves. Wray was the head coach, and Bell was his top assistant. But the pair also sold every ticket and served as the team's trainers. Bell couldn't afford a secretary, so he answered his own phone at the team's office.

The Eagles often played in front of sparse crowds during their early years.

Despite Bell and Wray's efforts, their team struggled. In 1933, the Eagles lost their first game 56–0 to the New York Giants. The blowout was a sign of things to come. Philadelphia didn't have a winning season in the 1930s.

With his team failing to attract talent, Bell came up with an idea that changed football forever. He got his fellow owners to agree on a draft of former college players coming into the league. The first draft was held in 1936, and Bell made the first pick. He chose quarterback Jay Berwanger from the University of Chicago. Berwanger wasn't long for Philadelphia, as Bell almost immediately traded him to the Chicago Bears. In the end, it didn't matter. Berwanger decided to skip the NFL altogether and became a salesman.

Though quarterback Jay Berwanger never played in the NFL, the Eagles made history by selecting him with the first-ever pick in the NFL Draft.

THE STEAGLES

By 1940, the Great Depression had ended. However, the United States soon faced another major challenge: In 1941, the country entered World War II (1939–1945). Many young men were drafted into the military. That left NFL teams, including the Eagles, short on talent.

In 1943, the Eagles' western Pennsylvania rivals, the Pittsburgh Steelers, had the same problem. The teams decided to combine their rosters for the season. Though they were officially known as "the Phil-Pitt Eagles," the one-year experiment is more commonly referred to as "the Steagles." It wasn't an easy situation. Each team had a player who thought they should be starting at each position. On top of that, Eagles coach Earle "Greasy" Neale had to co-coach with Pittsburgh's Walt Kiesling. The two often clashed over ideas.

Despite those tensions, the Steagles managed to put

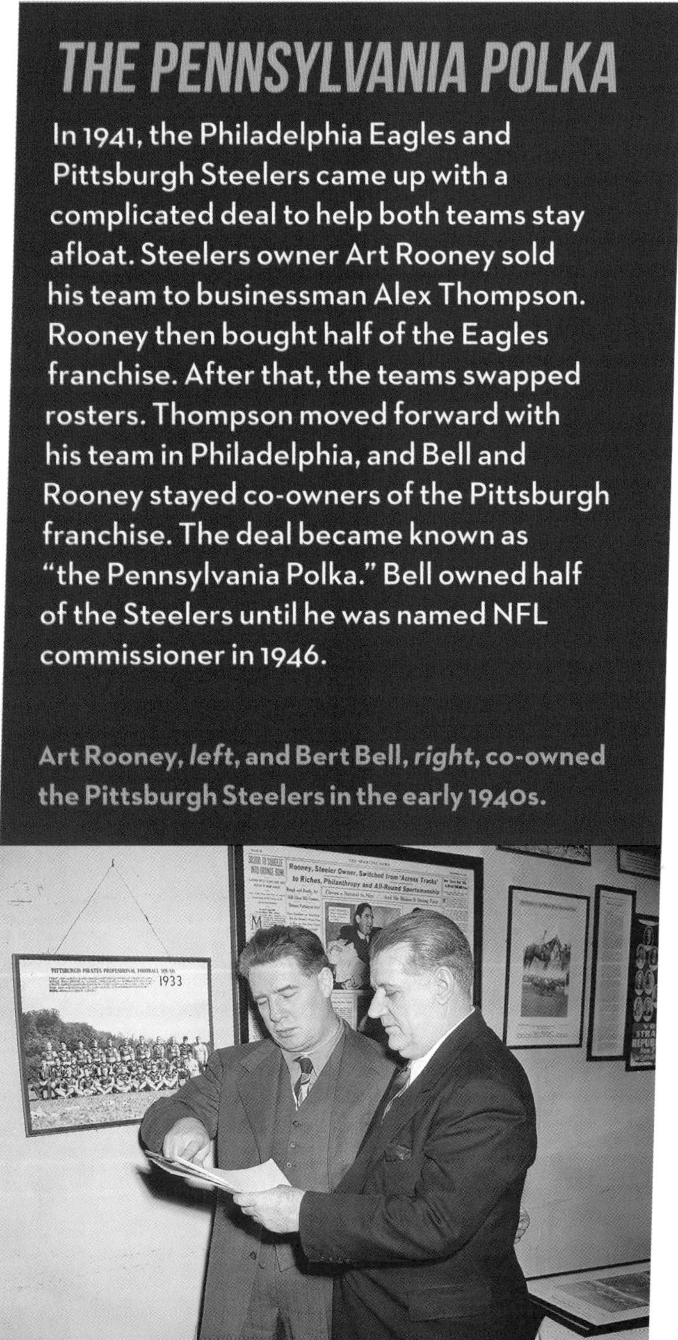

THE PENNSYLVANIA POLKA

In 1941, the Philadelphia Eagles and Pittsburgh Steelers came up with a complicated deal to help both teams stay afloat. Steelers owner Art Rooney sold his team to businessman Alex Thompson. Rooney then bought half of the Eagles franchise. After that, the teams swapped rosters. Thompson moved forward with his team in Philadelphia, and Bell and Rooney stayed co-owners of the Pittsburgh franchise. The deal became known as "the Pennsylvania Polka." Bell owned half of the Steelers until he was named NFL commissioner in 1946.

Art Rooney, *left*, and Bert Bell, *right*, co-owned the Pittsburgh Steelers in the early 1940s.

Greasy Neale won the 1919 World Series playing baseball for the Cincinnati Reds before winning two NFL titles as the Eagles' head coach.

together a winning season. The team finished the year with a 5-4-1 record. It was the first winning season in Eagles history.

POSTWAR BOOM

By 1946, World War II was over. Many soldiers who served overseas returned home ready to resume their usual lives. Veterans who had played elite football were eager to join or rejoin professional teams.

Neale signed several military veterans, and the Eagles' fortunes greatly improved in the late 1940s. Both quarterback Tommy Thompson and top receiver Pete Pihos had served in the army. In Philadelphia, the pair formed one of the best passing combinations in the NFL.

Thompson and Pihos were joined on offense by one of the era's most electrifying backs. Steve Van Buren stood 6 feet tall and weighed 200 pounds, which made him a big running back at the time. But his speed earned him the nickname "Supersonic Steve." Van Buren joined the Eagles in 1944 after the team drafted him fifth overall. By 1947, he was considered the best runner in football. Van Buren topped 1,000 yards for the first time in his career and led Philadelphia to the NFL Championship Game. There, the Chicago Cardinals found a way to stop the Eagles star. Holding Van Buren to just 26 yards, Chicago won 28–21.

Van Buren once again led the league in rushing in 1948. Thompson led the league by throwing 25 touchdown passes, including 11 to Pihos. The Eagles finished 9–2–1 and were set to host the NFL title game in a rematch against the Cardinals on December 19.

That day, a blizzard buried Philadelphia in several feet of snow. Van Buren, assuming the weather would force the game to be canceled, stayed home. Neale managed to get ahold of the star, and Van Buren

End Pete Pihos, *right*, caught 61 touchdown passes in nine seasons with the Eagles before leaving the team after the 1955 season.

raced to Philadelphia's Shibe Park, taking three trolleys and walking six or seven blocks in the heavy snow.

In such tough conditions, both teams struggled on offense. Thompson completed only two passes for 7 yards. The Cardinals weren't much better, throwing for only 35. The teams had a combined total of six turnovers. Despite his adventure getting to the stadium, Van Buren chugged through the snow for 98 rushing yards. But the game was still scoreless late in the third quarter. Then a Cardinals fumble gave Philadelphia the ball deep in Chicago territory. From 5 yards away, Van Buren plunged into the end zone three plays into the fourth quarter to win the game 7–0.

Van Buren (15) rushes through the snow in the 1948 NFL title game.

Less than a decade after struggling to field a team, the Eagles were NFL champions.

Nothing could slow Van Buren in 1949. The star back had his best season yet, rushing for league-leading totals of 1,149 yards and 11 touchdowns. The Eagles rolled to an 11–1 record and a third straight title game.

This time, the Los Angeles Rams hosted. Neale disliked flying, so the Eagles spent three days and three nights aboard a train from Philadelphia to the West Coast. The team arrived in Los Angeles to find the city soaked in rain.

With the field a mud pit, the teams' owners decided to postpone the game a week so more fans would show up. But Bell, then the NFL's commissioner, overruled them. As Philadelphia and Los Angeles slogged through the mud in front of just 22,000 fans, the only player who didn't seem to slow down was Van Buren. He carried the ball 31 times for a playoff record 196 yards. The only thing

From 1941 to 1950, Eagles quarterback Tommy Thompson threw for 10,385 yards and 91 touchdowns.

Van Buren didn't do was score. But Thompson and Pihos handled that when they connected on a 31-yard touchdown pass in the second quarter. Philadelphia's defense held down the Rams' feared passing attack. The Eagles added a second touchdown in the third quarter to win 14–0. The Eagles became just the second team since the advent of the NFL Championship Game in 1933 to win back-to-back titles. Nearly 80 years after those wins, Philadelphia remains the only team to post consecutive championship shutouts.

The Eagles, *in white*, held the Rams to just 119 total yards in the 1949 NFL title game.

Lineman Norm "Wild Man" Willey (86) played for the Eagles from 1950 to 1957. He reached two Pro Bowls with the team.

CHAPTER 3

ONE GREAT YEAR

The 1950 season was one of change in the NFL. As commissioner, Bert Bell had overseen the addition of three new teams from another league, the All-America Football Conference (AAFC). One of them was the Cleveland Browns, who had won the AAFC in each of the league's four seasons.

On opening night of the 1950 season, the Eagles hosted the Browns. Most people thought that the AAFC wasn't as good as the NFL. So many assumed that the Eagles would crush the Browns. Instead, Cleveland ran circles around Greasy Neale's team and won 35–10.

The loss signaled the end of the Eagles' short dynasty. The team slumped to 6–6 in 1950. At the time, the team was owned by a group of 100 investors headed by businessman

James Clark. "The Happy Hundred" fired the popular Neale after the season.

When Neale left, so did Philadelphia's winning ways. Under their next five head coaches, the Eagles failed to reach the NFL title game. By 1960, the team's successful days seemed like distant memories.

One of the Eagles' few highlights of the 1950s was quarterback Adrian Burk's seven touchdown passes against Washington on October 17, 1954.

CONCRETE CHARLIE

In the NFL's early years, many players played both offense and defense. That practice was dying out by the time Chuck Bednarik arrived in Philadelphia in 1949. Bednarik, however, became known as "the 60 Minute Man" because he often lined up at both center and middle linebacker.

Despite playing nearly every down on both offense and defense, Chuck Bednarik missed only three games in his 14-year career.

Over his 14 seasons, Bednarik developed a reputation as one of the most rugged players ever to wear an NFL uniform.

Bednarik's other nickname was "Concrete Charlie." Though he got it from his offseason job selling concrete, it also fit his on-field personality. Bednarik played the game with what he called "animal instincts." He was out to rough up his opponents before they did the same to him.

By 1960, Bednarik was mainly just playing offense. But when an early-season injury knocked out the team's middle linebacker, he went back to double duty. Playing nearly every down, Bednarik was an essential part of the Eagles as they put together a magical season.

Quarterback Norm Van Brocklin (11) helped turn the Eagles around after the team traded for him in 1958.

After losing their 1960 season opener, the Eagles reeled off nine straight victories. Quarterback Norm Van Brocklin paced the offense. One of the best passers of his era, Van Brocklin made his name with the Los Angeles Rams before joining the Eagles in 1958. By 1960, the 34-year-old quarterback found a connection with undersized receiver Tommy McDonald. The last NFL player to play without a facemask, the excitable McDonald caught 39 passes in 1960. He scored on 13 of them. Tight end Pete Retzlaff led the team with 46 catches and scored five times.

THE HIT

On November 10, the Eagles traveled to New York to face the powerhouse Giants. New York had won the NFL's East Division in three of the previous four seasons. But one play showed that the Eagles were ready to take the top spot.

Late in the game with the Eagles up 17–10, Giants running back Frank Gifford caught a pass while crossing over the middle of the field. Gifford was one of New York's biggest stars. Bednarik, coming the other way, leveled Gifford with a high hit. Gifford was knocked out and fumbled, and the Eagles recovered Gifford's fumble to seal their victory.

What became known simply as "the Hit" was controversial, especially after a photograph taken of the play appeared to show Bednarik taunting Gifford as the Giants' star lay on the ground. In fact, Bednarik said he was celebrating the fumble recovery. Gifford's injuries were so bad that he missed the entire 1961 season. But neither player ever thought it was a bad play. Gifford even later said,

Linebacker Chuck Bednarik (60) levels New York's Frank Gifford with "the Hit" in November 1960.

"Chuck hit me exactly the way I would have hit him. With his shoulder, a clean shot. That's football."

> ***"CHUCK HIT ME EXACTLY THE WAY I WOULD HAVE HIT HIM. WITH HIS SHOULDER, A CLEAN SHOT. THAT'S FOOTBALL."***
>
> **—FRANK GIFFORD**

WINNING IT ALL

The Eagles finished the 1960 season 10–2 to win the East Division. That set up an NFL title game matchup with the Green Bay Packers. The Eagles trailed 6–0 in the second quarter when Van Brocklin and McDonald brought the home crowd at Philadelphia's Franklin Field to its feet. McDonald broke open on the right sideline, and Van Brocklin hit his star receiver with a pass at the Green Bay 7. McDonald shrugged off a tackler and stumbled into the end zone for a 35-yard touchdown as the Eagles took a 7–6 lead.

Green Bay fought back and took a 13–10 lead with a touchdown early in the fourth quarter. But on the ensuing kickoff, Philadelphia running back Ted Dean raced 58 yards to the Packers' 39. Dean ended the drive by racing around the left end from 5 yards out to put the Eagles back up 17–13.

In the final seconds, the Packers drove deep into Philadelphia territory. Green Bay quarterback Bart Starr threw a pass to running back Jim Taylor, who was racing toward the Eagles' end zone when Bednarik slammed him to the turf at the 8 with less than 10 seconds left. The Packers were out of timeouts, and Bednarik smothered Taylor, not allowing the running back to get up. With their star stuck on the ground, the Packers couldn't get set for another play and time expired. After the clock ran out, Bednarik looked at Taylor and snarled, "You can get up now . . . This [game] is over."

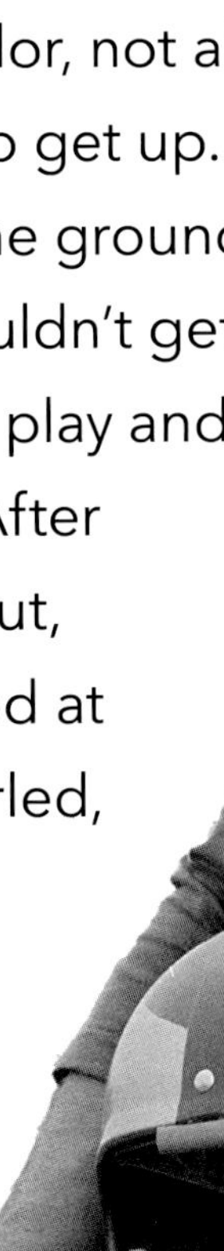

From 1957 to 1963, versatile athlete Tommy McDonald starred for the Eagles. During that time, he led the NFL in receptions twice.

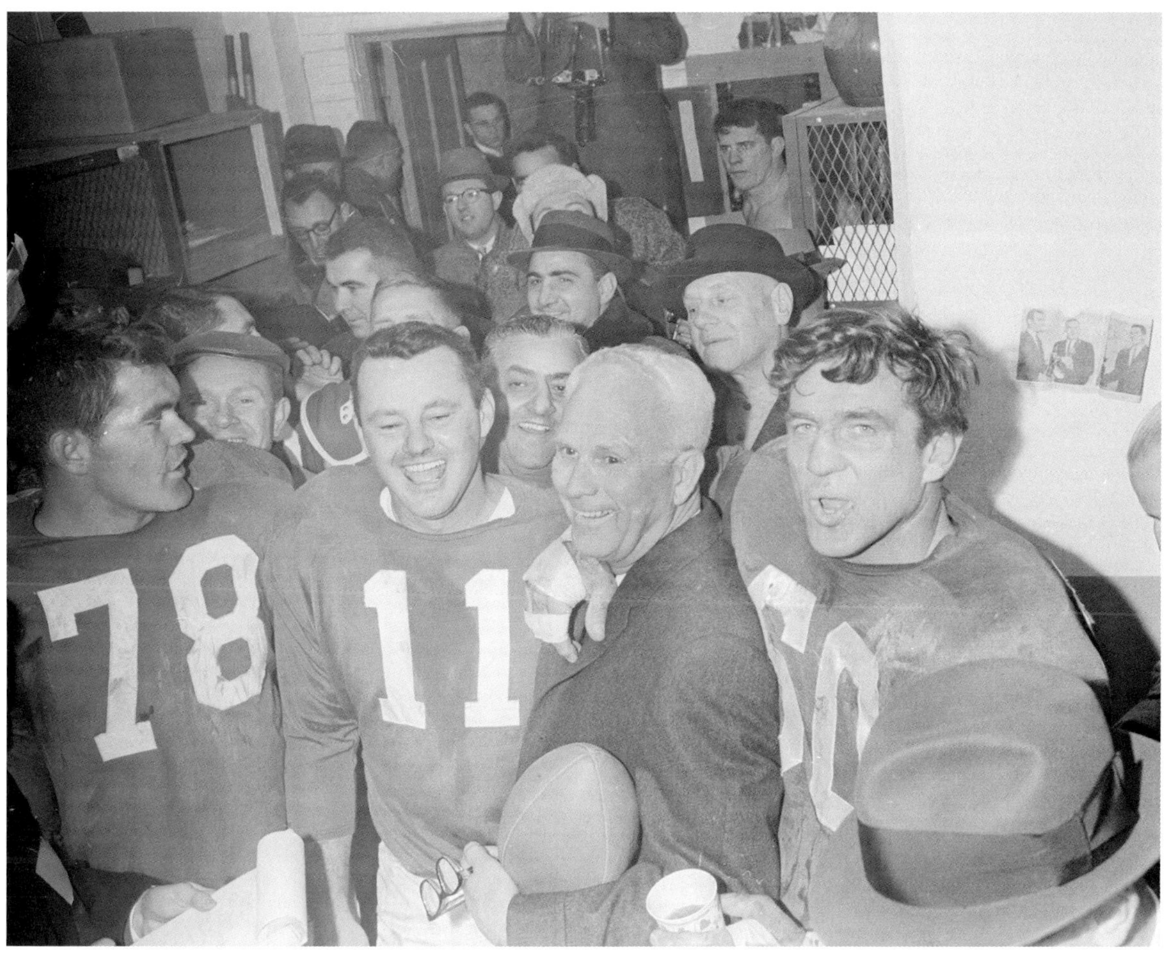

Eagles players celebrate with head coach Buck Shaw, *second from right*, after defeating the Packers in the 1960 NFL title game.

UNHAPPY TIMES

The Eagles' title was one of the most unexpected in NFL history. But their success didn't last. Both Van Brocklin and head coach Buck Shaw retired after the season. Bednarik played two more years. By the time Concrete Charlie left, the Eagles were in disarray. Feuding among the team's 100 owners was hindering the team, and the group eventually sold to local owner Jerry Wolman in 1963.

It didn't take long for Wolman to become one of the most unpopular owners in sports. He traded starting quarterback Sonny

Jurgensen to Washington in 1964, where he became a star. Wolman also signed off on a deal that sent McDonald to the Dallas Cowboys. Few players loved playing in Philadelphia more than McDonald, who nearly quit football when he found out he had been traded.

Eagles quarterback Sonny Jurgensen set a team record with 32 touchdown passes in 1961. The record stood until 2017.

SNOWBALLS FOR SANTA

On December 15, 1968, Eagles fans took out their frustrations in a strange way. It was the day after a snowstorm. With the team sitting at 2-11, the crowd was angry. At halftime, the Eagles had 20-year-old fan Frank Olivo take the field dressed as Santa Claus. As soon as he was introduced, the booing fans at Franklin Field began pelting Olivo with snowballs. The incident helped create the image of Philadelphia fans as some of the most unruly in the NFL.

A fan dressed as Santa Claus sits with other Eagles supporters at a game in 2024.

Wolman owned the Eagles until 1969 and oversaw only one winning season. By the end, the despised owner was bankrupt and forced to sell the team. New owner Leonard Tose took over. A former member of the Happy Hundred, Tose had a lot of work to do to bring joy back to Philadelphia football fans.

Leonard Tose, *right*, owned the Philadelphia Eagles from 1969 to 1984.

Dick Vermeil coached the Eagles from 1976 to 1982 and had a record of 54–47.

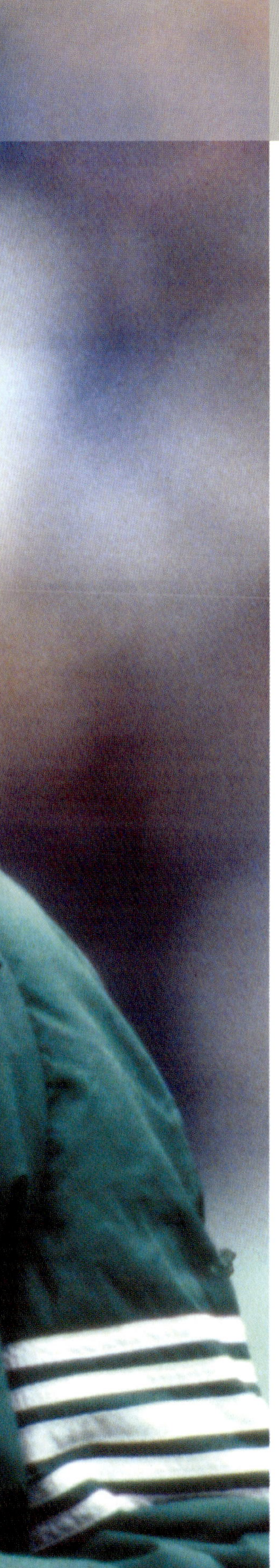

CHAPTER 4

REVIVAL

DICK VERMEIL WAS OBSESSED WITH FOOTBALL. THE ENTHUSIASTIC coach worked long days thinking of ways to make his teams better. When Philadelphia owner Leonard Tose hired Vermeil to coach his team in 1976, the owner was giving Eagles fans and players exactly what they needed.

In the losing years since the team's 1960 championship, Philadelphia fans had begun to wonder whether their team would ever win again. They still showed up to the team's new home, Veterans Stadium. But die-hard fans often did so to boo their struggling Eagles.

Vermeil was a breath of fresh air. Though he had never coached a professional team, he had been successful coaching on the college level. He cared deeply for his players on and off the field, which helped them endure his grueling practices.

THE MIRACLE AT THE MEADOWLANDS

One play signified the Eagles' turnaround under Dick Vermeil. In Week 12 of the 1978 season, the 6–5 Eagles traveled to face the 5–6 New York Giants. Late in the game, the Giants just needed to take a knee for a 17–12 victory. But New York called a running play and fumbled. Eagles defensive back Herman Edwards scooped up the ball and ran 26 yards for the winning touchdown. Eagles fans called the play "the Miracle at the Meadowlands." It was named after the area in which Giants Stadium was located. The 19–17 win helped Philadelphia clinch a playoff spot.

By 1978, the Eagles had a winning team. In his second year with the team, quarterback Ron Jaworski threw eight of his 16 touchdown passes to towering 6-foot-8-inch receiver Harold Carmichael. Running back Wilbert Montgomery rushed for a team-record 1,220 yards and nine scores. Veteran Bill Bergey led the defense. The Pro Bowl selection grabbed four interceptions that year.

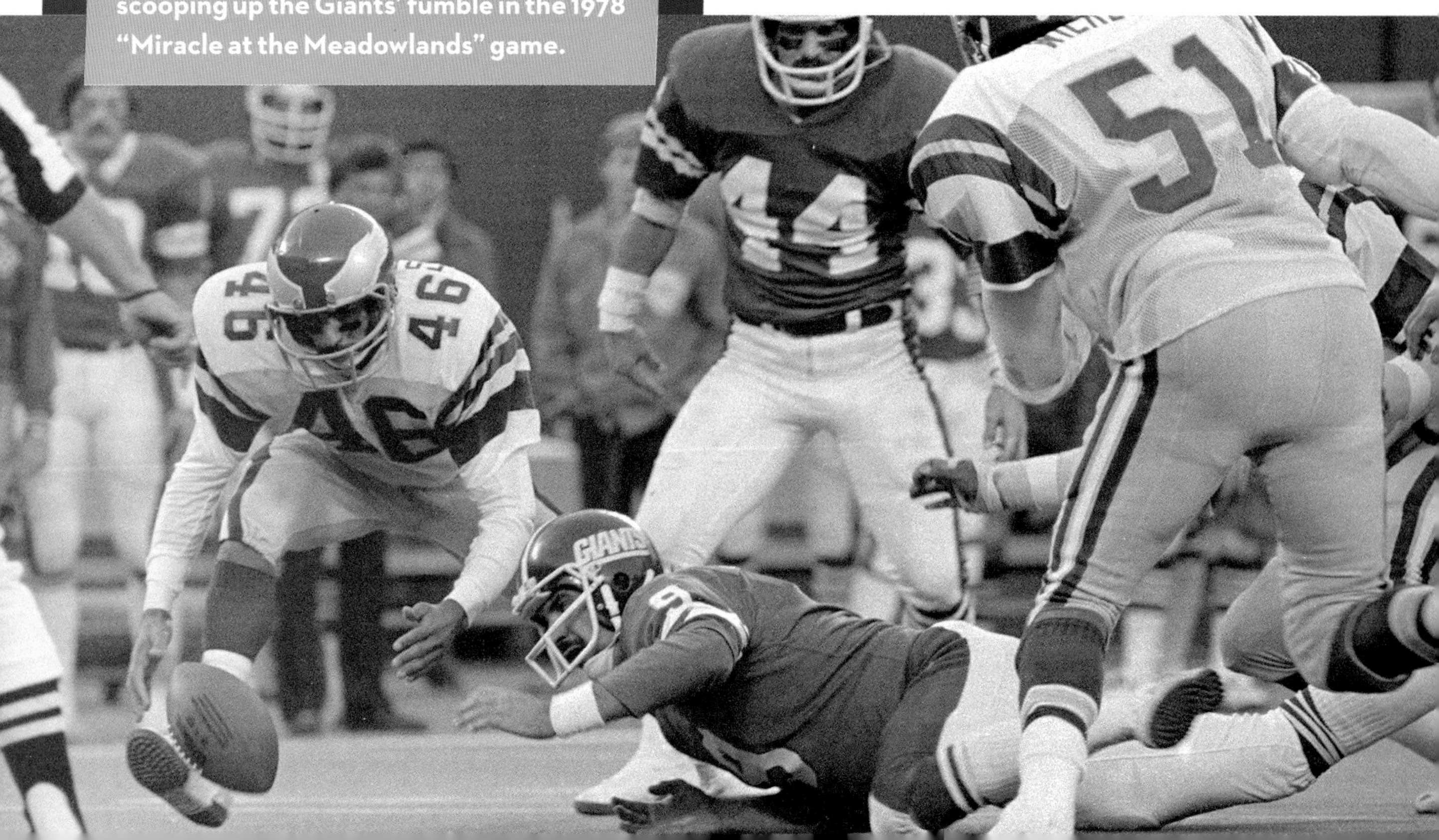

Eagles defensive back Herman Edwards, *left*, chases after the loose ball before scooping up the Giants' fumble in the 1978 "Miracle at the Meadowlands" game.

Running back Wilbert Montgomery left the Eagles in 1985 as the team's all-time leading rusher.

The Eagles rode a four-game winning streak in November to a 9–7 record and their first postseason appearance in 18 years. However, the Eagles blew a 13–0 lead to the Atlanta Falcons in the fourth quarter of the teams' wild-card round matchup and lost 14–13.

WHAT'S IT GOING TO TAKE?

One thing that Vermeil did for his team was give them an enemy to aim for. When Vermeil arrived, the Dallas Cowboys were one of the NFL's top teams. Philadelphia could never seem to beat the team, especially in Dallas. By 1979, the Eagles hadn't won a game in Dallas in 14 years. All season, Vermeil had been asking his players, "What is it going to take to beat the Dallas Cowboys?" It was a question he asked so often that his players got sick of hearing it. Vermeil even kept the Cowboys' statistics up on chalkboards in the Eagles' offices for the team to see.

Philadelphia traveled to Dallas for a key *Monday Night Football* game in Week 11. The Eagles had lost three straight games and needed a win. The night before the game, Vermeil gathered his players and asked them again, "What's it going to take to beat the Dallas Cowboys?" The players were silent, so Vermeil answered himself. "Another 24 hours," he said, and left the room. The fired-up Eagles won 31–21, sparking a winning streak that drove the team to the playoffs. Philadelphia beat the Chicago Bears in the wild-card round. But the following week, the Eagles fell to the Tampa Bay Buccaneers and their season was over.

Eagles linebacker Bill Bergey (66) and teammate John Bunting wrap up a Dallas Cowboys runner in 1980.

SUPER EAGLES

By 1980, the Eagles were an elite team. Their defense allowed the fewest points in the league. Jaworski threw a career-high 27 touchdown passes. The Eagles finished 12–4 and won their division for the first time in two decades.

After routing the Minnesota Vikings 31–16 in the divisional round of the playoffs, the Eagles hosted the Cowboys at Veterans Stadium in the conference title game. The temperature was in the single digits, with 30-mile-per-hour (48 km/h) winds, but the Eagles felt the warmth of the fans they had won over. Jaworski said later, "When we came down that tunnel and heard the fans, it was 70 degrees and sunny."

"WHEN WE CAME DOWN THAT TUNNEL AND HEARD THE FANS, IT WAS 70 DEGREES AND SUNNY."

—RON JAWORSKI

It was Dallas's eighth trip to the conference title game in 11 years. But the Eagles showed no intimidation. After the Eagles stuffed the Cowboys' first drive, Jaworski handed the ball to Montgomery on Philadelphia's second offensive play. Battling knee injuries, Montgomery had played only 12 games all season. But he burst through a hole on the right side and sprinted 42 yards for the opening touchdown. Philadelphia's defense did the rest, holding the Cowboys to just 206 yards and forcing four turnovers. The Eagles won 20–7 and advanced to Super Bowl XV.

Eagles quarterback Ron Jaworski prepares to throw a pass during Super Bowl XV on January 25, 1981.

Philadelphia entered the Super Bowl as favorites to beat the Oakland Raiders. But the Eagles played their worst game of the season. Jaworski threw three interceptions, all to Oakland linebacker Rod Martin, and the Eagles' offense never got going. Oakland won 27–10.

Vermeil guided the Eagles for only two more seasons. The now 46-year-old coach worked such long hours that he often slept in his office. After the team missed the playoffs in 1982, the coach gave a tearful press conference announcing his resignation, saying, "I'm physically and emotionally burned out."

Wide receiver Harold Carmichael left the Eagles in 1984 as the team's all-time leader in receptions, yards, and touchdowns.

BUDDY BALL

The aging Eagles went through many changes in the early 1980s. The team's Super Bowl stars had all moved on or retired. But by the middle of the decade, a new group of fan favorites took over. Philadelphia drafted quarterback Randall Cunningham in 1985. Cunningham was one of the few Black starting quarterbacks of his era. His blend of passing and running skills amazed fans. Cunningham used his long, graceful strides to chew up yardage on the ground. From 1987 to 1990,

Eagles quarterback Randall Cunningham scrambles for yardage in a game against the New York Giants in 1992.

Cunningham was the Eagles' leading rusher and one of the league's best passers. Along the way, he picked up the nickname "the Ultimate Weapon."

While Cunningham provided thrills on offense, the Eagles became one of the league's scariest defensive teams. Philadelphia had a defensive roster of young, physical players. Linebacker Seth Joyner and safety Andre Waters were fierce hitters. Up front, Jerome Brown, Clyde Simmons, and Reggie White shut down quarterbacks. White was the star of "the Green Gang." Off the field, the 6-foot-5, 291-pound defensive end was an ordained minister. But for the Eagles, "the Minister of Defense" was the NFL's best pass rusher. White was named First-Team All-Pro every year from 1986 to 1991. In 1987, he racked up a league-high 21 sacks to become the NFL's Defensive Player of the Year.

Philadelphia defensive end Reggie White recorded 21 sacks in 1987 despite playing only 12 games that year.

The other component of the Eagles' fierce defense was the team's new head coach. Buddy Ryan took over in 1986 after a long career as one of the game's best defensive coordinators. Ryan was one of the most divisive coaches in NFL history. His players loved his aggressive style, but opposing teams and fans often accused Ryan of poor sportsmanship and coaching his teams to play dirty.

Under Ryan, the Eagles went back to the playoffs in 1988 and took on the Chicago Bears in the wild-card round. In one of the strangest games in NFL history, Chicago's Soldier Field was blanketed with a thick layer of fog. Players struggled to see one another, and fans in the stands could barely make out what was happening. Though Cunningham managed to top 400 passing yards, the Eagles never reached the end zone and lost "the Fog Bowl" 20–12.

In 1989, Ryan caused a controversy when the team traveled to Dallas on Thanksgiving to take on the Cowboys. After the Eagles' 27–0 win, stories surfaced that Ryan had offered his players bonuses

The Eagles and the Bears battle through a heavy fog during the playoffs on December 31, 1988.

for big hits on Dallas quarterback Troy Aikman and kicker Luis Zendejas. "The Bounty Bowl" overshadowed the Eagles' 11-5 season. However, once again the team was eliminated in their first playoff game.

In 1990, Ryan fanned more flames. Before a game against Washington on *Monday Night Football*, the coach told reporters that the Eagles would not only win but would also physically dominate their rivals. The Eagles did win, 28–14, but many viewers were horrified by the fact that Washington lost six players to injury, including both quarterbacks. The team had to finish the game with running back Brian Mitchell playing under center. Washington got the last laugh, though. When the teams met in the playoffs, Washington won 20–6.

That playoff loss was Ryan's last game as the Eagles' head coach. After five seasons of controversy and zero playoff wins, Ryan was fired. The change didn't help much. The Eagles reached the playoffs only three more times in the 1990s.

The team's best playoff memory of that decade came

Buddy Ryan was one of the NFL's most controversial coaches.

Philadelphia quarterback Rodney Peete threw for a career-high 2,326 yards in 1995.

after the 1995 season. Philadelphia faced the Detroit Lions in the wild-card round. Before the game, Detroit tackle Lomas Brown said that there was no way his team would lose. By halftime, Philadelphia quarterback Rodney Peete had thrown two touchdown passes as the Eagles built a 38–7 lead. In front of a roaring crowd at Veterans Stadium, Philadelphia won 58–37. But the Eagles couldn't build off that momentum. The next week, Philadelphia lost 30–11 to their rivals, the Cowboys.

Eagles receiver Rob Carpenter, *center*, celebrates a touchdown catch with teammates Fred Barnett, *left*, and Chris Jones during the Eagles' 58–37 win over the Lions in the playoffs on December 30, 1995.

In 11 seasons with the Eagles, quarterback Donovan McNabb set team records for passing yardage and touchdowns.

CHAPTER 5

SOARING EAGLES

The Eagles entered the 1999 draft with the second overall pick. They chose quarterback Donovan McNabb. Eagles fans loudly booed the pick. They thought the team should have chosen another athlete. But McNabb soon won them over. Working with new coach Andy Reid, McNabb led the Eagles back to the playoffs in his second season. A solid passer and skilled runner, McNabb was named runner-up for the league's Most Valuable Player Award. The Eagles reached the playoffs after each of the next three seasons. McNabb continued his strong play with help from running back Duce Staley. Middle linebacker Jeremiah Trotter and safety Brian Dawkins paced a fierce, hard-hitting defense.

Despite the Eagles' success, reaching the Super Bowl proved tough. Philadelphia reached the NFC title game after the 2001 season and lost to the St. Louis Rams 29–24. A year later, the Eagles fell to the Tampa Bay Buccaneers 27–10 in the NFC Championship Game. In 2003, Philadelphia's offense was shut down by the Carolina Panthers in a 14–3 NFC title-game defeat.

BREAKING THROUGH

By 2004, the Eagles were tired of finishing runners-up in the NFC. Reid's team featured McNabb, dual-threat running back Brian Westbrook, and star receiver Terrell Owens. The defense allowed just 16.3 points per game that regular season.

The Eagles won 13 games for the first time in team history despite losing Owens to an ankle injury in December. But McNabb and the defense took over in the playoffs. After McNabb threw two touchdown passes in a 27–14 divisional-round win over the Minnesota Vikings, the Eagles faced the Atlanta Falcons in the NFC title game. The Falcons were led by Michael Vick, who was

FOURTH-AND-26

The Eagles trailed the Packers 17–14 with 1:12 left in the divisional round of the 2003 playoffs. Even worse, Philadelphia faced fourth-and-26 at its own 26-yard line. Quarterback Donovan McNabb heaved a desperation pass over the middle to receiver Freddie Mitchell. Mitchell caught the pass 1 yard short of the first down, then battled through two tacklers to reach the line. The miracle play set up a game-tying field goal from kicker David Akers. Philadelphia then won the game 20–17 in overtime.

the league's most dangerous running quarterback. But the Eagles sacked the speedy Vick four times. Dawkins added a key interception in the third quarter, and Philadelphia won 27–10.

That win sent the Eagles to Super Bowl XXXIX to face the defending-champion New England Patriots. With Owens back in the lineup, McNabb threw for 357 yards. But he also fired three interceptions in a narrow 24–21 defeat.

Running back Brian Westbrook rushed for more than 6,000 yards with the Eagles from 2002 to 2009. He also caught 442 passes.

Eagles safety Brian Dawkins, *left*, returns the ball behind linebacker Jeremiah Trotter after Dawkins's interception in the NFC title game on January 23, 2005.

SOMETHING SPECIAL

Reid stayed on as Philadelphia's coach through the 2012 season. He became the Eagles' all-time winningest coach but couldn't get Philadelphia back to the Super Bowl. Despite star performances from shifty running back LeSean McCoy and speedy receiver DeSean Jackson, Philadelphia reached the postseason only once between 2011 and 2016.

Andy Reid won 130 games as coach of the Eagles from 1999 to 2012.

Entering the 2017 season, Philadelphia fans had newfound optimism. Head coach Doug Pederson had built a talented offense around new quarterback Carson Wentz. Wentz had 33 touchdown passes in the team's first 13 games. But a knee injury in Week 14 knocked him out for the season.

Fans were worried Wentz's injury would

sink the Eagles. Philadelphia's backup was Nick Foles, who had been drafted by the Eagles in 2012 and started several games for the team in his first three seasons. But since being traded in 2015, he had bounced around the NFL before returning to the Eagles to back up Wentz.

Foles played well, and the Eagles finished 13–3. Philadelphia knocked off the Falcons 15–10 in the divisional round. Foles then threw three touchdowns in a 38–7 rout over the Vikings to put the Eagles into Super Bowl LII against the New England Patriots.

Even though Foles had a hot hand heading into Super Bowl LII, most observers thought the Patriots would roll in the championship game. New England was the defending champion, and it still had Tom Brady, the quarterback who had beaten the Eagles in Super Bowl XXXIX after the 2004 season. At age 40, Brady was seeking his sixth Super Bowl victory.

With 38 seconds left in the first half, Philadelphia held a 15–12 lead. The Eagles faced fourth down from the Patriots 1-yard line. Pederson called timeout to make a plan. Foles came over to the

Quarterback Carson Wentz had already broken the Eagles' single-season record for touchdown passes when he was injured in 2017.

Eagles quarterback Nick Foles leans in to talk to coach Doug Pederson before "the Philly Special" in Super Bowl LII on February 4, 2018.

sideline and said, "You want Philly Philly?" Pederson paused for a moment and looked at his quarterback. "Yeah, let's do it," the coach replied. Foles nodded and jogged back to the huddle.

"Philly Philly" was a play also called "the Philly Special." The team had never run it in a game before. Foles lined up in the shotgun formation. He then wandered toward the line and pretended to call an audible. As he did, center Jason Kelce snapped the ball to running back Corey Clement. Clement pitched the ball on a reverse to tight end Trey Burton. As the Patriots raced to figure out what was happening, Foles slipped undetected into the end zone. The quarterback was wide open as Burton flipped a touchdown pass to Philadelphia's quarterback. Both the crowd at US Bank Stadium in Minneapolis and the Patriots were stunned by the gutsy call. The play became one of the most famous in Super Bowl history. Pederson said later, "It's one of those moments where you're like, this is the moment that's going to win you the Super Bowl."

"IT'S ONE OF THOSE MOMENTS WHERE YOU'RE LIKE, THIS IS THE MOMENT THAT'S GOING TO WIN YOU THE SUPER BOWL."

—DOUG PEDERSON

The game was far from over. The Patriots rallied to take a 33–32 lead with 9:22 left. Foles coolly led a 14-play drive that cut through New England's defense. On third-and-seven from the New England 11-yard line, tight end Zach Ertz broke over the middle. Foles zipped a pass on target. Ertz hauled it in, then dived over a fallen defender for a touchdown. The Eagles missed the two-point conversion but still held a 38–33 lead with 2:21 to play.

Foles reaches out to haul in Trey Burton's touchdown pass in Super Bowl LII.

Up until that point, the game had been all offense. The teams ended up with a combined 1,151 total yards, more than any other NFL game ever played. But the Eagles' defense stepped up when it mattered most.

Philadelphia tight end Zach Ertz dives in with the go-ahead touchdown late in Super Bowl LII.

On New England's second play of the next drive, Philadelphia defensive end Brandon Graham raced around his blocker and swatted the ball loose from Brady. The fumble bounced straight to the Eagles' other defensive end, Derek Barnett. The key recovery led to a field goal from kicker Jake Elliott. The Patriots' last-ditch Hail Mary fell incomplete, and the Eagles were finally champions.

NEW HEIGHTS

The celebration of Super Bowl LII didn't last long in Philadelphia. Foles left the team after the 2018 season. While Wentz threw for more than 4,000 yards and 27 touchdowns in 2019, Philadelphia lost in the wild-card round. In 2020, the Eagles won only four games, and Pederson was let go.

The Eagles picked quarterback Jalen Hurts in the second round of the 2020 NFL Draft.

Alongside aggressive general manager Howie Roseman, new coach Nick Sirianni quickly rebuilt the Eagles as an electrifying offensive team. By 2022, new quarterback Jalen Hurts was surrounded with weapons. Receivers A. J. Brown and DeVonta Smith had a combined total of 18 touchdown receptions. Hurts rushed for more than 700 yards and 13 touchdowns. Running back Miles Sanders added 11 more along with 1,269 yards on the ground.

Philadelphia could beat teams in many ways. One of the most unique was the team's approach to short-yardage plays. The team lined up for a standard quarterback sneak, but with a twist. Multiple players would line up behind Hurts, then throw their bodyweight into him after the snap to force him forward. In a nod to Philadelphia's slogan as "the City of Brotherly Love," the play became known as "the Brotherly Shove." It was also called

The Eagles execute "the Brotherly Shove" in a 2023 game against the Buffalo Bills.

"the Tush Push." The play was nearly unstoppable. Soon other teams began to copy Philadelphia's strategy.

The Eagles finished 14–3, then got through the playoffs to set up an exciting matchup in Super Bowl LVII against the Kansas City Chiefs. The game had many intriguing storylines. Kelce was playing against his younger brother, Travis, a star tight end for the Chiefs. It was the first time two brothers ever played against each other in the Super Bowl. Hurts and Kansas City's Patrick Mahomes made history as the first two Black quarterbacks to start the same Super Bowl.

The two stars delivered a thriller. Hurts threw a touchdown pass and rushed for three more. But Mahomes got the ball last with the game tied 35–35. He led the Chiefs on a final drive to sink the Eagles 38–35 on a field goal with eight seconds left.

Defensive tackle Fletcher Cox recorded 70 sacks in 12 seasons with the Eagles before retiring in 2024.

The Eagles took a step back in 2023, but Roseman and Sirianni never stopped looking for ways to improve the team. Before the 2024 season, they added another elite offensive weapon. They signed star running back Saquon Barkley away from the rival Giants. Barkley proved to be the missing piece. He wowed the NFL by rushing for 2,005 yards and 13 touchdowns. The league's Offensive Player of the Year then added 442 yards and five touchdowns in three playoff games as the Eagles set up a Super Bowl rematch with the Chiefs.

EAGLES TROPHY CASE

SUPER BOWL CHAMPIONSHIPS: 2

Super Bowl LII – February 4, 2018
Super Bowl LIX – February 9, 2025

NFL CHAMPIONSHIPS: 3

1948, 1949, 1960

CONFERENCE CHAMPIONSHIPS: 4

1980, 2004, 2022, 2024

DIVISION TITLES: 17

NFL East: 1947, 1948, 1949, 1960
NFC East: 1980, 1988, 2001, 2002, 2003, 2004, 2006, 2010, 2013, 2017, 2019, 2022, 2024

All stats are through the 2024 season.

Eagles running back Saquon Barkley shows off his athleticism by hurdling over a Jacksonville Jaguars defender in 2024.

Kansas City found a way to slow down Barkley in the title game. The Eagles' star runner picked up just 57 yards. But Philadelphia's defense pounded Kansas City. In a dominant performance, Philadelphia routed the Chiefs 40–22. Once again, the Eagles were soaring above the rest of the NFL.

TIMELINE

1933
The Eagles are founded by owner Bert Bell.

The Eagles, combined with the Pittsburgh Steelers, experience their first winning season.
1943

1948
On December 19, Philadelphia wins its first NFL championship by beating the Chicago Cardinals 7-0 in a blizzard.

Led by star running back Steve Van Buren, Philadelphia beats the Los Angeles Rams 14-0 to win the NFL title.
1949

Behind the inspired play of center and linebacker Chuck Bednarik, the Eagles win their third NFL title.
1960

1981
On January 25, coach Dick Vermeil leads Philadelphia to its first Super Bowl, but the team falls 27-10 to the Oakland Raiders.

Buddy Ryan is fired as Philadelphia's coach after five controversial seasons with the team.
1991

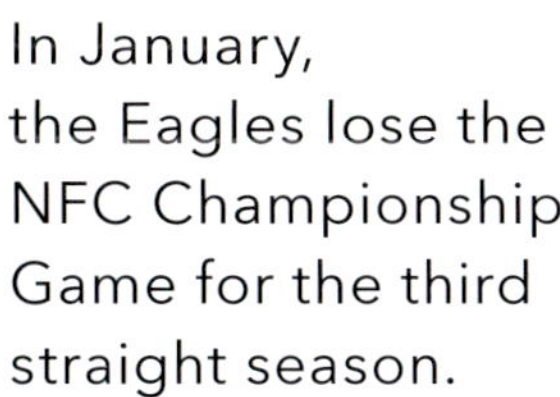

In January, the Eagles lose the NFC Championship Game for the third straight season.

2004

2005

On February 6, coach Andy Reid and quarterback Donovan McNabb lead Philadelphia to the Super Bowl where the Eagles lose 24–21 to the New England Patriots.

2018

Behind "the Philly Special," the Eagles defeat New England 41–33 in Super Bowl LII on February 4.

2023

On February 12, Philadelphia's high-powered offense leads the team to Super Bowl LVII, where the Eagles lose 38–35 to the Kansas City Chiefs.

After finishing 14–3 in the 2024 season, the Eagles rout the Kansas City Chiefs 40–22 to win Super Bowl LIX on February 9.

2025

GLOSSARY

audible—when the quarterback changes the play at the line of scrimmage after seeing how the defense has lined up.

bankrupt—unable to pay debts.

clinch—when a team secures something, such as a win or a playoff berth.

commissioner—the chief executive of a sports league.

coordinator—an assistant coach who is in charge of the offense, defense, or special teams.

draft—a system that allows teams to acquire new players coming into the league.

dynasty—a team that has an extended period of success, usually winning multiple championships in the process.

era—a period of time in history.

franchise—an entire sports organization.

general manager—an executive who runs a team and is responsible for finding and signing players.

Hail Mary—a long pass that has a small chance of succeeding, usually made near the end of a game as a last-ditch effort to score.

momentum—the strength or force that allows something to continue or to grow stronger.

pick six—an interception returned for a touchdown.

postseason—another word for playoffs; the time after the end of the regular season when teams play to determine a champion.

retire–to end one's career.

rival–an opponent with whom a player or team has a fierce and ongoing competition.

sack–a tackle of the quarterback behind the line of scrimmage before he can pass the ball.

turnover–loss of the ball to the other team through an interception or fumble.

veteran–someone who has played for many years.

wild-card–the first round of the playoffs.

ONLINE RESOURCES

To learn more about the Philadelphia Eagles, please visit **abdobooklinks.com** or scan this QR code. These links are routinely monitored and updated to provide the most current information available.

INDEX